AF408722

TO MY FELLOW VISUAL LEARNERS

and Brad♡

doodled Definitions

by Jillian Dickson

 B.O.W. Publishing

ALTERITY

al-**teh**-ruh-tee

noun

THE STATE OF BEING OTHER OR DIFFERENT; OTHERNESS.

ACATALEPSY

ey-**kat**-l-ep-see
noun

THE IMPOSSIBILITY TO UNDERSTAND THE UNIVERSE OR ARRIVE AT
FULL COMPREHENSION.

CHURLISH

chur-luhsh
adjective

RUDE, BOORISH, MEAN-SPIRITED.

ARMISTICE

aar-muh-stuhs
noun

AGREEMENT BY OPPOSING SIDES IN A WAR TO STOP FIGHTING.

ULTRACREPIDARIAN

uhl-truh-krep-eh-deh-ree-uhn
noun or *adjective*

EXPRESSING OPINIONS ON MATTERS OUTSIDE THE SCOPE OF ONE'S
KNOWLEDGE OR EXPERTISE.

FACEBOOK

STEATOPYGIA

stee-a-tuh-**pi**-jee-uh
noun

EXTREME ACCUMULATION OF FAT ON THE BUTTOCKS.

INEFFABLE

i-**neh**-fuh-bl
adjective

TO GREAT OR EXTREME TO BE EXPRESSED OR DESCRIBED IN
WORDS.

UMBRAGE

uhm-bruhj
noun

TAKE OFFENSE AT, ANGERED BY.

PYRRHIC

pee-ruhk
adjective

VICTORY THAT COMES AT TOO GREAT OF A COST.

WE WON

AESTHETE

es-theet
noun

A PERSON WITH SPECIAL APPRECIATION OF ART AND BEAUTY.

SUBTERFUGE

suhb-tr-fyooj
noun

A TRICK OR A DISHONEST WAY OF ACHIEVING SOMETHING.

ANECDOCHE

ah-**nek**-dah-kee

noun

A CONVERSATION WHEREIN EVERYONE IS TALKING BUT NOBODY
IS LISTENING.

MY
WAY
MY
OPINION
MY
IDEAS
MY
WAY

JOUSKA

jow-ska
noun

A HYPOTHETICAL CONVERSATION THAT YOU COMPULSIVELY PLAY
OUT IN YOUR HEAD.

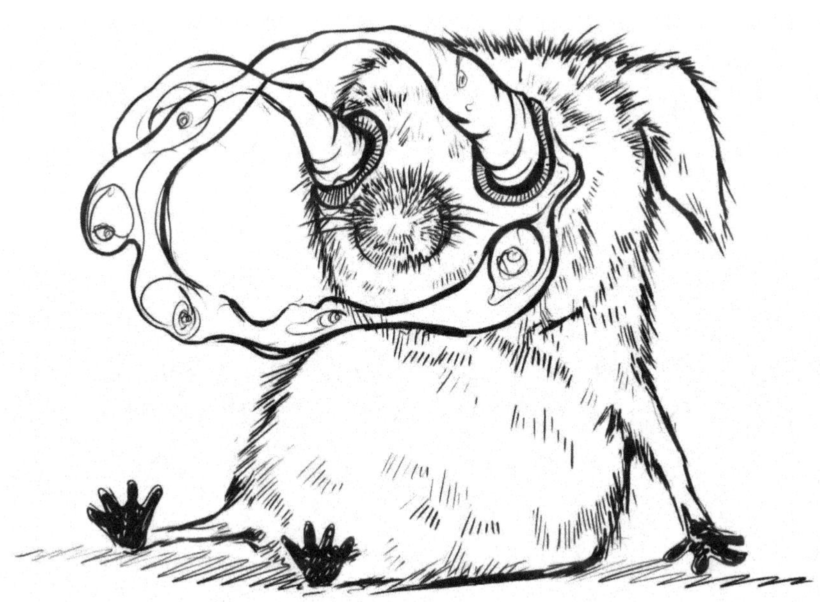

CALUMNY

ka-luhm-nee
noun

MAKING FALSE AND DEFAMATORY STATEMENTS ABOUT
SOMEONE IN ORDER TO DAMAGE THEIR REPUTATION.

GRUBBLE

gruh-bul
verb

TO FEEL OR GROPE IN THE DARK.

CONTIGUOUS

kuhn-**ti**-gyoo-uhs
adjectiive

SHARING A COMMON BOARDER, TOUCHING.

HELIOPHILE

heel-ee-oh-fai-uhl

noun

ONE ATTRACTED OR ADAPTED TO SUNLIGHT.

ATARAXIA

a-tr-**ak**-see-uh
noun

CALMNESS UNTROUBLED BY MENTAL OR EMOTIONAL
ANXIETY OR WORRY.

Home

BEGUILE

buh-**gile**
verb

CHARM, ENCHANT, INFLUENCE BY TRICKERY.

GROK

graak
verb

UNDERSTANDING SOMETHING INTUITIVELY OR BY EMPATHY.

240'
240'

GAUCHE

gowsh

adjective

LACKING EASE OR GRACE, UNSOPHISTICATED AND SOCIALLY
AWKWARD.

UNMOORED

uhn-**mord**
adjective

INSECURE, CONFUSED, LACKING CONTACT WITH REALITY.

ULOTRICHOUS

yoo-**lah**-tri-kuhs
adjective

HAVING WOOLY OR CRISPY CURLY HAIR.

HYGEE

hyoo-guh
noun

COZINESS AND COMFORT THAT ENDGENDERS CONTENTMENT.

EXPERGEFACTOR

ek-purg-**fak**-tr
noun

SOMETHING THAT WAKES YOU UP IN THE MORNING.

APRICITY

ay-**pris**-ity

noun

THE WARMTH OF THE SUN IN THE WINTER.

EQUANIMITY

ee-kwuh-**ni**-muh-tee

noun

COMPOSURE, MENTAL CALMNESS, ESPECIALLY IN A DIFFICULT SITUATION.

SOLIPSISM

saa-luhp-si-zm
noun

THE VIEW THAT THE SELF IS ALL THAT CAN BE KNOWN TO EXIST.

ASTROPHILE

as-**trow**-fai-uhl

noun

A PERSON WHO LOVES STARS.

GESTICULATE

jeh-**sti**-kyuh-layt
verb

EXPRESSING MEANING WITH GESTURES.

CAPACIOUS

kuh-**pay**-shuhs
adjective

SPACIOUS, ROOMY.

BOWDLERIZE

bowd-lr-ize
verb

REMOVE MATERIAL THAT IS CONSIDERED IMPROPER OR OFFENSIVE, ESPECIALLY WITH THE RESULT THAT THE TEXT BECOMES WEAKER OR LESS EFFECTIVE.

CENSOR

DISSEMBLE

duh-**sem**-bl
verb

CONCEAL ONE'S TRUE MOTIVES, FEELINGS.

TIMOROUS

ti-mr-uhs
adjective

SHOWING NERVOUSNESS, FEARFUL, LACKING CONFIDENCE.

INSOUCIANCE

uhn-**soo**-see-uhns

noun

BEING INDIFFERENT OR UNCONCERNED.

AHHH!

FELICITY

fuh-**li**-suh-tee
noun

INTENSE HAPPINESS.

FATUOUS

fa-choo-uhs
adjective

SILLY, POINTLESS, FOOLISH, AIRHEADED.

TENUOUS

teh-nyoo-uhs
adjective

THIN, SLENDER, WEAK, SLIGHT, INSUBSTANTIAL

SUPINE

soo-pine
adjective

LYING FACE UPWARDS.

GELID

geh-luhd
adjective

ICY, EXTREMELY COLD.

MISANTHROPE

mi-suhn-throwp
noun

A PERSON WHO DISLIKES HUMANKIND AND AVOIDS HUMAN
SOCIETY.

EMPATHIC

em-**pa**-thuhk
adjective

SHOWING THE ABILITY TO UNDERSTAND AND SHARE THE FEELINGS OF ANOTHER.

BUS

PUGNACIOUS

puhg-**nay**-shuhs
adjective

EAGER OR QUICK TO ARGUE, QUARREL, OR FIGHT.

NEFARIOUS

nuh-**feh**-ree-uhs
adjective

WICKED, VILLAINOUS.

MERCURIAL

mr-**kyur**-ee-uhl

adjective

SUBJECT TO SUDDEN OR UNPREDICTABLE CHANGE OF MOOD.

PRESCIENT

preh-shee-uhnt
adjective

HAVING OR SHOWING KNOWLEDGE OF EVENTS BEFORE THEY
TAKE PLACE.

FUTURE

LIMERENCE

li-mr-uhns
noun

STATE OF BEING INFATUATED OR OBSESSED WITH ANOTHER PERSON.

GORGONIZE

gor-guh-nize
verb

TO HAVE A PARALYZING OR MESMERIZING EFFECT,
STUPIFY, PETRIFY.

PARITY

peh-ruh-tee

noun

THE STATE OR CONDITION OF BEING EQUAL, ESPECIALLY
REGARDING STATUS OR PAY.

IMBROGLIO

uhm-**brow**-lee-ow
noun

COMPLICATED, CONFUSING, EMBARASSING SITUATION.

NEMOPHILIST

nee-**mow**-fee-list

noun

SOMEONE WITH A LOVE OR FONDNESS FOR FORESTS.

INTRANSIGENT

in-**tran**-suh-jnt
adjective

UNWILLING OR REFUSING TO CHANGE ONE'S VIEWS OR AGREE
ABOUT SOMETHING.

IN GOD WE TRUST

GRAVITAS

graa-vuh-taas
noun

DIGNITY, SERIOUSNESS, OR SOLEMNITY OF MANNER.

NIRVANA

nr-**vaa**-nuh

noun

TRANSCENDENT STATE, NO MORE SUFFERING, A STATE OF OBLIVION TO CARE.

RESPLENDENCE

ri-**splen**-duhns
noun

DAZZLING BEAUTY, BRILLIANCE.

BELLICOSE

beh-luh-kows
adjective

DEMONSTRATING AGGRESSION AND WILLINGNESS TO FIGHT.

MAGNUM OPUS

mag-nuhm-**ow**-puhs
noun

THE GREATEST ACHIEVEMENT OF AN ARTIST.

TACITURN

ta-suh-trn
adjective

RESERVED, SAYING LITTLE, DECLINED TO TALK.

SELCOUTH

sel-kooth
adjective

ODD, UNUSUAL, STRANGE.

PANACEA

pa-nuh-**see**-uh

noun

A REMEDY FOR ALL THINGS.

MERAKI

meh-ruh-kai
noun

DOING SOMETHING WITH SOUL.

HERALD

heh-ruhld
noun

AN OFFICIAL MESSENGER BRINGING NEWS.

NAUGHTY
NICE

PSITHURISM

sith-yuh-riz-uhm
noun

THE SOUND OF LEAVES AS WIND BLOWS THROUGH TREES.

MELLIFLUOUS

muh-**li**-floo-uhs
adjective

SMOOTH, RICH SOUND.

PETRICHOR

peh-truh-kor
noun

PLEASANT SMELL AFTER SUMMER RAIN.

AEOLIST

e-oh-list
noun

A POMPOUS PERSON PRETENDING TO HAVE INSPIRATION OR
SPIRITUAL INSIGHT.

PULCHRITUDINOUS

puhl-kruh-**too**-duh-nuhs
adjective

BREATHTAKING, HEARTBREAKING BEAUTY.

BUCOLIC

byoo-**kaa**-luhk
adjective

PLEASANT ASPECT OF RURAL LIFE.

HELLO

EVANESCENT

eh-vuh-**neh**-snt
adjective

FLEETING, FADING OR DISAPPEARING QUICKLY.

ESURIENT

uh-**sur**-ee-uhnt
adjective

HUNGRY, GREEDY.

FUDGEL

fuh-jul
verb

TO PRETEND TO WORK WHEN IN REALITY ONE IS NOT DOING
ANYTHING.

CACOETHES

cac-o-e-thes

noun

AN IRRESISTIBLE URGE TO DO SOMETHING INADVISABLE.

OBFUSCATE

aab-fuh-skayt
verb

RENDER OBSCURE, UNCLEAR, CONFUSE.

TRUTH

PAROXYSM

peh-ruhk-si-zm
noun

SUDDEN ATTACK OF AN EMOTION OR ACTIVITY.

CYNOSURE

sai-now-shr

noun

ONE WHO IS THE FOCUS OF ADMIRATION, CENTER OF ATTENTION.

EFFERVESCENT

eh-fr-**veh**-snt
adjective

BUBBLY, VIVACIOUS, ENTHUSIASTIC.

EFFLUVIUM

uh-**floo**-vee-uhm
noun

A SLIGHT OR INVISIBLE EXHALATION OR VAPOR, ESPECIALLY ONE THAT IS DISAGREEABLE OR FOUL SMELLING.

DENOUEMENT

day-noo-**maan**

noun

THE FINAL PART OF A PLAY, MOVIE, OR NARRATIVE IN WHICH THE STRANDS OF THE PLOT ARE DRAWN TOGETHER AND MATTERS ARE RESOLVED OR EXPLAINED.

LASSITUDE

la-suh-tood
noun

PHYSICAL OR MENTAL WEARINESS, LACK OF INTEREST, ENERGY, SPIRIT.

Published by   B.O.W. Publishing

Pictures copyright 2024 by Jillian Dickson

Library of Congress Cataloging - in Publication Data

Summary: A collection of obscure words, their definition, and an illustration to better understand the meaning. Designed for folks who are visual learners.

ISBN 979-8-218-32684-5

Drawings and Design by Jillian Dickson
Text in Times New Roman

The illustrations were created with ink pen on paper